Adventures in Cartooning

ACTIVITY BOOK

James Sturm
Andrew Arnold
Alexis Frederick-Frost

:01
First Second
New York & London

Ugh, rain is **SO** boring.

It's **RUINING** my life!

Poof

What? Who?!

It's me, the Magical Cartooning Elf! Why so glum, chum?

Elf!

I'm bored out of my **MIND!** There's nothing fun to do.

6

I like those doodles but I want something EXCITING.
How about a monster? Or an evil wizard?! Or a GIANT?!!
Let's draw them!

DRAW HERE!

Psst! The knight hasn't checked the dining room table yet. Draw Edward by the table.

15

The monster is growing larger by the second. The panels show him growing over time. How big does he get? You decide, and draw him in the last panel.

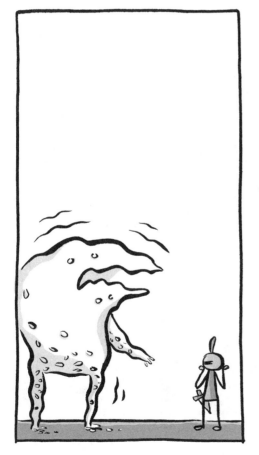

18

Draw Edward and the knight escaping the Cookie Monster. To show how fast they are going, add motion lines or little puffs of dirt!

MOTION LINES

PUFFS OF DIRT

The knight is excited because he defeated the Cookie Monster.

HOORAY!

What is the knight saying?

 The Magic Chef likes to make a big exit. Use sound effects to give his magic a little extra excitement!

 Add a: POOF!

 Add a: BANG!

 Add a: CRACK!

The knight and Edward wonder what is making all the noise in the library. Draw their ideas in their thought bubbles.

WHAT COULD IT BE?

A jackhammer?

A dog? BARK! BARK! BARK!

A volcano? BOOM!

The giant is sleeping soundly in his recliner. Draw the rest of the giant here.

MODEL SHEET

Comics need to be read from left to right, top to bottom.*

On the next page, redraw these panels in the right order so they make sense.

* Except for Japanese comics!

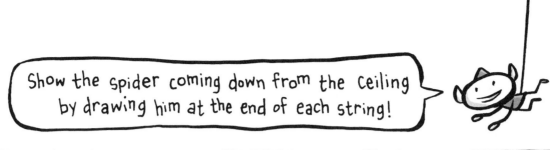

Add backgrounds to the panels below to change these tiny insects into **GIANT CREATURES!**

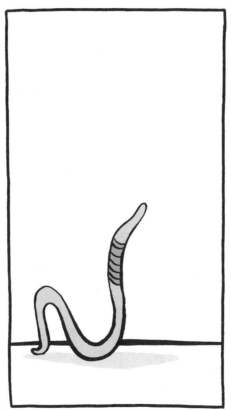

The giant's hair is messy because he just woke up from a nap...
What do you look like when you wake up?

1. After a good night's sleep.

2. After taking a nap.

3. After getting **NO** sleep at all.

Edward and the knight bumped their heads pretty hard. So hard, that they are dazed and confused.
Draw birds, stars, or scribbles to show they are loopy.

Draw what's hiding in the shadows!

WHAT COULD IT BE?

 bats?

 snakes?

 spiders?

Draw your own robot heads using the parts below.

ROBOT PARTS

The more panels you use, the longer something takes. It took the knight four panels to complete the robot. Can you draw the knight completing the robot in just two panels?

Now it's your turn!
Use the blank panels on the following pages to make your own comic. Here are some cartooning tools you can use:

Comics are made up of **PANELS**.
A panel shows a moment in time.

The more panels you have, the longer something takes.

BACKGROUNDS

Create a sense of scale by adding backgrounds.

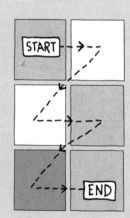

Comics are read from **LEFT** to **RIGHT**, **TOP** to **BOTTOM**.

WORD BALLOONS
show what a
character is saying.

THOUGHT BALLOONS
show what a character is
thinking.

The way a word
balloon is shaped
can change what
it means.

SCREAM!

But the most
important thing
to keep in mind
is to...

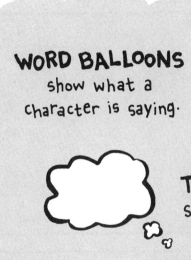

WHISPER

HAVE
FUN!

Start your comic by using this large panel to show where it takes place.

Once upon a time...

64

65

69

THE END

First Second

New York & London

Published by First Second
First Second is an imprint of Roaring Brook Press, a division of Holtzbrinck Publishing Holdings Limited Partnership
175 Fifth Avenue, New York, New York 10010

Distributed in Canada by H.B. Fenn and Company Ltd.
Distributed in the United Kingdom by Macmillan Children's Books, a division of Pan Macmillan.

Cataloging-in-Publication Data is on file at the Library of Congress

ISBN: 978-1-59643-598-8

First Second books are available for special promotions and premiums.
For details, contact: Director of Special Markets, Holtzbrinck Publishers.

First Edition
August 2010
Printed in June 2010 in the United States of America by RR Donnelley & Sons Company, New York

10 9 8 7 6 5 4 3 2 1

BY ART
WE LIVE